FUNNY BONE TiCKLeRS iN VeRSE aND RHYME

Selected by
Leland B. Jacobs

Drawings by
Edward Malsberg

GARRARD PUBLISHING COMPANY
CHAMPAIGN, ILLINOIS

Library of Congress Cataloging in Publication Data
Jacobs, Leland Blair, 1907-
  Funny bone ticklers in verse and rhyme.
  (Reading shelf-poetry)
  SUMMARY: Humorous verses by various poets describe
strange animals, people, and events and ask silly
questions.
  1. Children's poetry. [1. Humorous poetry.
2. Nonsense verses] I. Malsberg, Edward, illus.
II. Title.
PZ8.3.J138Fs   808.81'8   73-3178
ISBN 0-8116-4115-5

The editor and publisher acknowledge with thanks permission received to reprint the poems in this collection.

Acknowledgments and formal notices of copyright for all
material under copyright appear on page 61, which is hereby
made an extension of the copyright page.

Contents

Hippopotamusses

Hippopotamusses never
Put on boots in rainy weather.
To slosh in mud up to their ears
Brings them great joy and merry tears.
Their pleasure lies in being messed up.
They just won't play at being dressed up.
In fact a swamp is heaven plus
If you're a hippopotamus.

Arnold Spilka

From . . .

Bears Are Better Left Alone

If you should ask a bear to tea
What would you give your guest to eat?
You'd hesitate if you were me
To offer him a hunk of meat,
For he might grow too greedy—he
Might add his hostess to his tea!

Elizabeth Coatsworth

Only My Opinion

Is a caterpillar ticklish?
    Well, it's always my belief
That he giggles, as he wiggles
    Across a hairy leaf.

                    Monica Shannon

I Know a Camel

I know a camel who paints the enamel
    Of all of his teeth a bright blue.
When I asked him why, he declared with a sigh,
    "I'd tell you if only I knew!"

                    Edward Anthony

The Ambiguous Dog

The dog beneath the cherry tree
Has ways that surely puzzle me:

Behind, he wags a friendly tail;
Before, his growls would turn you pale!

His meaning isn't plain and clear!
Oh, is the wag or growl sincere?

I think I'd better not descend;
His bite is at the growly end.

Arthur Guiterman

The Giraffe's Breakfast

The giraffe has a neck
Which stretches so high
That sometimes I think
It can reach to the sky.

From his mouth to his tummy
Is such a long way,
His meals have to travel
For hours each day.

A giraffe would enjoy
His breakfast much more
If he started to eat it
The evening before.

Ilo Orleans

Advice About Lions

Should a lion come to call,
Do not venture in the hall,
Do not lift the latch at all.

When he rings and rings your bell,
Stay inside and all is well.

He's probably a hungry lion,
So he'll keep tryin',
He'll keep tryin'.

Lee Blair

Supper for a Lion

Savage lion in the zoo,
Walking by on padded feet,
To and fro and fro and to,
You seem to think it's time to eat.

Then how about a bowl of stew
With jello for dessert? Or would
A juicy bone be best for you?

Oh, please don't stare
   As though you knew
      That I'd taste good!

Dorothy Aldis

An Explanation of Porcupines

Like cactus plants,
    All porcupines,
Protect themselves
    With quills and spines
So sharp and horrid
    To the touch
You would not like them
    Very much.

Merlin Millet

The Centipede

    A centipede
    Has a hundred legs
With which to move about;
    And traveling
    Around, for him,
Is an easy task, no doubt.

    But if I were
    A centipede
I'm sure I wouldn't know
    In what direction,
    Right or left,
My legs would want to go!

Ilo Orleans

Birthday Cake

If little mice have birthdays
(and I suppose they do)

And have a family party
(and guests invited too)

And have a cake with candles
(it would be rather small)

I bet a birthday CHEESE cake
would please them most of all.

Aileen Fisher

The Busy Gardener

"Stop bothering us!" said the cutting worms,
And the beetle bugs, and the sleepy moles.
"It's much too early in the spring for you
To dig up houses the way you do!"

"If I'm a bother—I beg your pardon,"
The gardener said. "But I'm digging a garden.
A garden without any stones or stumps,
Of good, soft earth without any lumps—
A garden where carrot seeds will grow,
And little green peas in a viney row,
And tasty herbs, and crisp wax beans,
And radishes, too, and salad greens—
So that's how it is. I'm digging a garden,
And if it annoys you—I beg your pardon."

"No trouble at all!" cried the cutting worms,
And the beetle bugs, and the hungry moles.
"We're in *your* way, sir! We'll all be going—
But we'll all be back
    When you get things
            growing!"

Kathryn Jackson

Puzzlement

There came into a barber shop
    A beaver and a bear.
The barber took one look at them,
    And said, "I do declare,
In all my days I've never seen
    A more peculiar pair.
I don't know which of them to shave,
    And which to cut his hair."

Kay Dee

Futile Old Gentleman

There was an Old Man who supposed
That the street door was partially closed;
    But some very large rats
    Ate his coats and his hats
While that futile Old Gentleman dozed.

Edward Lear

Silly Old Man

There was an old man in a garret,
    Who was so afraid of a rat,
That he pulled himself up to the ceiling,
    And hung himself up in his hat.

Old Rhyme

Betty Botter

Betty Botter bought some butter,
"But," said she, "this butter's bitter.
When I put it in my batter,
It makes all my batter bitter."
So she bought some better butter,
And put it in the bitter batter,
To make the bitter batter better.

Old Rhyme

What a Girl!

There's a girl who lives with the Brands
Whom nobody understands.
    Not to muddy her feet
    When she crosses the street,
She goes across on her hands.

Jay Lee

Florinda Fury

When Florinda Fury went to town
She always wore a bear-skin gown,
And when she wanted to look her best,
For a hat she'd wear an eagle's nest.

Ennis Rees

Sir Mortimer Burt

In olden days, when knights rode forth,
To keep from getting hurt
They all wore armor, all except
The bold Sir Mortimer Burt.

Said Sir Mortimer Burt
(Also known as the Fearless),
"Armor? I cannot abide it
I'd rather be bruised
By a blow from without
Than from bumping around
       When inside it!"

Kathryn Jackson

Amazon Sleeper

A sleeper from the Amazon
Put nighties of his gra'mazon—
 The reason that
 He was too fat
To get his own pajamazon.

Unknown

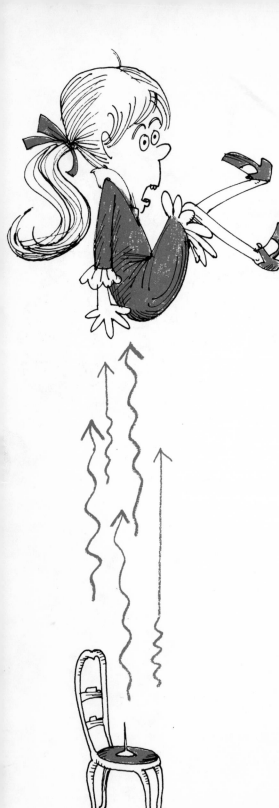

Maggie Rose

You'd do the same
    As Maggie Rose.
You'd be no different,
    I suppose.
For when she sat
Upon a tack,
    Maggie Rose.

Unknown

Lily Wood

Her name was Lily Wood,
    My son,
And be that as it should;
When asked if rich she'd like to be,
She answered, "Lily Wood."

Her name was Lily Wood,
    My son,
And be that as it should.
When asked if Queen she'd like to be,
They learned that Lily Wood.

Unknown

Tickle, Tickle

At a picnic old Mrs. Cryder
Happened to swallow a spider,
   Her neighbors now say
   She laughed all the next day,
'Cause the spider kept tickling insider.

Elbee Jay

In an Onion Bed

A worker
in an onion bed
cried and wept
and sadly said:
"I'd like to find
an onion bed
where I can
smile and laugh
instead."

Lee Blair

The Shutter Shutter

A chap by the name of Cutter
Did well at shutting a shutter.
   So shutters he shut,
    And shut, shut, and shut
Till they couldn't be shut any shutter.

Unknown

Leslie More

A neighbor whom we all called Les,
Although his name is Leslie More,
Unnoticed moved away, I guess.
We found this news tacked on his door:
    No Les
    No More.

Anonymous

Owen More

Did you ever hear
    This tale before
About that chap
    Named Owen More?

Well, Owen More,
    He went away
Owen More
    Than he could pay.

He just came back
    From some far shore.
I hear he still is
    Owen More.

Unknown

Odd Old Men

There was an old man in Waterloo
Who always put spinach in his stew.

There was an old man in Albert Lea
Who mixed his coffee with his tea.

There was an old man in Uniontown
Who gobbled pickled pumpkins down.

There was an old man in Pleasantville
Who spiced his apple pie with dill.

There was an old man at Rambling Lake
Who sprinkled catsup on his cake.

There was an old man in East Malone
If you want a last line, you must write your own!

Anonymous

Supper Talk

"I hope it isn't
Too impolite,
But what will you have
To eat tonight?"
Asked Mrs. White.

"Oyster stew,"
Said Mrs. Drew.

"Pizza pie,"
Said Mrs. Blye.

"Brown baked beans,"
Said Mrs. Means.

"Roast of pork,"
Said Mrs. York.

"Macaroni,"
Said Miss Maloney.

"Whipped cream cake,"
Said Mrs. Blake.

"Now, what are you having,
Mrs. White?"

"Only a bite,
Only a bite,
I'm dieting,"
Said Mrs. White.

Jay Lee

Hopper

That girl named Natalie Hopper
Was always a clippity-clopper.
    She hopped on the stair,
     In the square, everywhere,
And nobody ever could stopper.

B. J. Lee

Gossip

Did I tell you
    About Polly Plockett,
Who carried pudding
    In her pocket?

I'll tell you something
    Even worse.
Jane has jello
    In her purse.

And I can tell you
    Something too.
Sue has a suitcase
    Full of stew.

Well, I've got nothing
    Like that to share.
I just have gum
    Stuck in my hair.

Merlin Millet

The Merry Pieman's Song

"You are the cake of my endeavor, and my jelly-roll
    forever;
My tapioca tartlet, my lemon-custard pie;

You're my candied fruit and spices, my juicy
    citron slices;
You're the darling, sugar-sprinkled apple-
    dumpling of my eye!"

John Bennett

The Terrybird's Song

The Terrybird
In rainy weather,
If he gets wet,
He dries each feather,
And as he does,
He sings this song,
"I'm glad I brought
My towel along."

Kay Dee

Sailor Song

I've been across the ocean blue,
    I've been across the sea,
And, oh, you are the fairest maid,
    So won't you marry me?

I'll give you oceanfuls of love,
    I'll very well behave,
And go to sea no more, if you
    Will be my permanent wave!

B. J. Lee

Runaway Song

I'm running away to Timbuctoo,
Where I can do what I want to do,
With no more eating what's on my plate,
And no more going to bed at eight,
And no more washing before each meal,
And no more "Stops!" if I shout or squeal,
And no more need to try to explain
How my shoes got wet when there was no rain,
Or why in the cat's tail there was glue,
So I'm running away to Timbuctoo.

Lee Blair

Lumberjack Ballad

Oh, I jumped into a river.
    It wasn't very deep,
But it had a solid bed whereon
    I quickly went to sleep.

Oh, I jumped into a river,
    Because it had a bed,
And it had a sheet of water
    For to cover up my head.

Oh, I jumped into a river.
    I slept soundly till the sun
Woke me up, and then the ripples
    Said, "It's time for you to run."

Oh, I jumped into the river,
    And I jumped back out again,
And I recommend its bunk house
    To all tired and sleepy men.

Unknown

Sing Me a Song

Sing me a song about a fox.

> A fox put on
> His shoes and sox
> And went to visit
> His friend, the ox,
> Tra-lee, Tra-la, Tra-lox.

Sing me a song about a bear.

> A bear put on
> His underwear
> And went to visit
> His friend, the hare,
> Tra-lee, Tra-la, Tra-lare.

Sing me a song about a goat.

    A goat put on
    His pants and coat,
    And went to visit
    Another goat,
      Tra-lee, Tra-la, Tra-loat.

Sing me a song about a gnu.

    A gnu put on
    One Sunday shoe
    And went to visit
    I don't know who,
      Tra-lee, Tra-la, Tra-loo.

Sing me a song about a bee.

    A bee put on—
    O, deary me—
    I've run out of song,
    As you can see,
      Tra-lee, Tra-la, Tra-lee.

          Merlin Millet

Vegetables

A carrot has a green fringed top;
    A beet is royal red;
And lettuces are curious,
    All curled and run to head.

Some beans have strings to tie them on,
    And, what is still more queer,
Ripe corn is nothing more or less
    Than one enormous ear!

But when potatoes all have eyes,
    Why is it they should be
Put in the ground and covered up—
    Where it's too dark to see?

Rachel Field

Lids

It's good we have eyelids
that close at a touch
to keep out an insect
or sun that's too much.
Why don't we have EARlids
for thunder and such?

Aileen Fisher

Snail's Pace

Maybe it's so,
That snails are slow,
They trudge along,
And tarry.

But isn't it true,
You'd slow up, too,
If you had your home
To carry?

Aileen Fisher

I Ask You

I'd like to ask you the question
    I often think about:
Whatever does a firefly do
    When its batteries burn out?

B. J. Lee

Sleep

When I can't get myself to sleep
It always helps when I count sheep.
If a little sheep can't sleep, does he
Get sleepy counting boys like me?

Gino Bell-Zano

A Little Girl's Question

Twinkle, twinkle, little star,
Let me ask you what you are:
Are you a diamond in the sky
That the Lady Moon can buy?
And if a diamond you should be,
How much would one like you cost me?

Merlin Millet

The Answer

What would your answer be,
    What would you say
Of a fat man who ate
    Forty waffles a day—
Who ate forty waffles,
    That greedy old man?
What would you say?
    Tell me quick as you can!
HOW WAFFLE!

Kay Dee

Peep in the Basket

Peep in the basket,
What do you see?
Five little kittens—
And one is for me!

Five little kittens—
Which one shall I choose?
The gray one that's purring?
The white one that mews?

The all-over black one?
The black with white paws?
The tigery-striped one?
I can't choose because—

Each one, when I pet it,
Seems surely the best.
So—could you keep the basket—
And give me the rest?

Kathryn Jackson

Did You Hear?

Did you hear
Of the snail
Who, on getting his mail,
Read all of the ads
But the "Houses for Sale"?

Did you hear
Of the crow
Who was learning to sew,
And hemstitched designs
On a blanket of snow?

Did you hear
Of the deer
Who, when quite filled with fear,
Jumped so high and so far
She was into next year?

B. J. Lee

Fuzzy Wuzzy

Fuzzy Wuzzy was a bear.
Fuzzy Wuzzy had no hair.
So Fuzzy Wuzzy wasn't fuzzy,
    Was he?

Unknown

Topsy-Turvy Turnabouts

The Error

A man once put his dog to bed,
    Then shut *himself* out in the dark.
He didn't discover the error he'd made
    Till he chased a car and couldn't bark.

Ennis Rees

Turnabout

There was an old ghost all in white
Who frightened the townsfolk at night,
    And when he'd appear,
    They'd cry out in fear,
Which filled the old ghost with delight.

But when light—be it ever so dim—
Came back to the heaven's broad rim,
    When once there was sun,
    The ghost was undone,
For the townspeople then frightened him!

B. J. Lee

The Town of Upside Down

There is a funny kind of town
Where everything is upside down
   And stands upon its head.
At night the children run and play,
And then as soon as it is day,
   They all go straight to bed.

What do you think they have to eat?
Marshmallow cake and berries sweet,
   Whipped cream and Easter eggs.
And when they dine in that queer town,
They turn the tables upside down
   And sit among the legs.

No dog is bigger than a pup,
But children there are born grown up
   And never need obey.
The clothes they wear are never new.
The parents always have to do
   Just what the children say.

Georgia MacPherson

Tim's Trained Catfish

Tim trained a catfish to live on dry land,
    Till at last it followed him around.
But out in a boat with Tim one day,
    The fish fell overboard and drowned.

Ennis Rees

From . . .

The Walrus and the Carpenter

The sun was shining on the sea,
    Shining with all his might:
He did his very best to make
    The billows smooth and bright—
And this was odd, because it was
    The middle of the night.

The moon was shining sulkily,
    Because she thought the sun
Had got no business to be there
    After the day was done—
"It's very rude of him," she said,
    "To come and spoil the fun!"

Lewis Carroll

The Rabbit Hunt

Three men went hunting rabbits
Last winter in the fall,
One could not hear, one could not see,
One could not move at all.

The deaf one heard the rabbit first,
The blind one stalked his trail,
The one who could not move jumped up
And caught him by the tail.

Jack Prelutsky, translator

Ducks

A man taught his ducks to swim in hot water,
    Which made them squawk and churn their legs,
But the idea worked, as sure it ought'o,
    For now they lay nothing but hard-boiled eggs.

Ennis Rees

Difficult Name

A man had such a difficult name
    He'd almost always wreck
At least a dozen pens or so
    Whenever he signed a check.

Ennis Rees

Jack and Willie

Jack and Willie of New Orleans
    Are very lazy boys.
To sneeze, Jack tosses back his head,
    Then Willie makes the noise.

Ennis Rees

Stella's Telescope

Stella has a telescope
    That's hard to understand.
It brings the birds so close to her
    She pats them with her hand.

Ennis Rees

Two Arizona Gunmen

Two Arizona gunmen,
    At some poor man's expense,
While practicing shot all the barbs
    Off a barbwire fence.

Then loading up their guns,
    With powder, barbs, and glue,
They shot the barbs back on again.
    I can show the fence to you!

Ennis Rees

Acknowledgments

Abelard-Schuman, Ltd., New York: For "Lids" and "Birthday Cake" by Aileen Fisher. Reprinted from *Runny Days, Sunny Days* by Aileen Fisher. By permission of Abelard-Schuman, Ltd. All Rights Reserved. Copyright year 1958 by Aileen Fisher. For "Florinda Fury," "Two Arizona Gunmen," "Ducks," "Tim's Trained Catfish," "Stella's Telescope," "Jack and Willie," "The Error," and "Difficult Name" by Ennis Rees. Reprinted from *Tiny Tall Tales* by Ennis Rees. By permission of Abelard-Schuman, Ltd. All Rights Reserved. Copyright year 1967 by Ennis Rees.

Abelard-Schuman, Ltd., London: For "The Rabbit Hunt" from *No End of Nonsense* by Jack Prelutsky, published by Abelard-Schuman, Ltd., Great Britain. © Abelard-Schuman 1970.

American Education Publications: For "Snail's Pace" by Aileen Fisher. Special permission granted by *My Weekly Reader,* Issue 32, Vol. 47, published by Xerox Publications, © Xerox Corporation, 1970.

John H. Bennett, Jr.: For "The Merry Pieman's Song" by John Bennett from *The Pigtail of Ah Lee Ben Loo* by John Bennett. Reprinted by permission of John H. Bennett, Jr., Administrator, D.B.N., C.T.A., of the estate of John Bennett.

Doubleday & Company, Inc.: For "I Know a Camel" by Edward Anthony from the book *Oddity Land,* copyright © 1957 by Edward Anthony. For "Vegetables" by Rachel Field from the book *Taxis and Toadstools* by Rachel Field, copyright 1926 by Doubleday & Company, Inc. For "Only My Opinion" by Monica Shannon from *Goose Grass Rhymes* by Monica Shannon, copyright 1930 by Doubleday & Company, Inc. Reprinted by permission of Doubleday & Company, Inc.

Exposition Press, Inc.: For "The Town of Upside Down" by Georgia MacPherson from *Little Poems for Little People* by Georgia H. MacPherson, © 1949 by Georgia H. MacPherson. Used by permission of the publisher, Exposition Press, Inc.

Vida Lindo Guiterman: For "The Ambiguous Dog" from *Lyric Laughter* by Arthur Guiterman. Reprinted by permission of Vida Lindo Guiterman, who owns the copyright. Published by E. P. Dutton and Company, Inc.

The Instructor Publications, Inc.: For "Sleep" by Gino Bell-Zano. Reprinted from the *Instructor,* © April 1968, The Instructor Publications, Inc. Used by permission.

Freide Orleans Joffe: For "The Centipede" and "The Giraffe's Breakfast" by Ilo Orleans from *The Zoo That Grew* by Ilo Orleans published by Henry Z. Walck, Inc. By permission of Freide Orleans Joffe.

Macmillan Publishing Co., Inc.: For "The Rabbit Hunt" by Jack Prelutsky. Reprinted with permission of Macmillan Publishing Co., Inc., from *No End of Nonsense* by Jack Prelutsky. Copyright © 1966, 1968 by Gerhard Stalling Verlag. For "Bears Are Better Left Alone" by Elizabeth Coatsworth. Reprinted with permission of Macmillan Publishing Co., Inc., from *Summer Green* by Elizabeth Coatsworth. Copyright 1948 by The Macmillan Company.

Henry Z. Walck, Inc.: For "Hippopotamusses" by Arnold Spilka from *A Lion I Can Do Without,* copyright © 1964 by Arnold Spilka. Used by permission of Henry Z. Walck, Inc., publisher.

Western Publishing Company, Inc.: For "Peep in the Basket," "Sir Mortimer Burt," and "The Busy Gardener" by Kathryn Jackson from *The Golden Bedtime Book* by Kathryn Jackson, © 1955 by Western Publishing Company, Inc.

Index
of Authors